To

From

Words to Warm a Teacher's Heart
© 2009 Summerside Press
www.summersidepress.com

Compiled by Joanie Garborg
Designed by Jenny Bethke

ISBN 978-1-934770-51-1

Printed in China

WORDS TO WARM
A
Teacher's
HEART

TABLE OF CONTENTS

. . . .

God Made Teachers Special	5
The Light of Understanding	11
Dreaming of Great Things	17
Entrusted with the Future	23
Press On	29
A Work of Heart	35
To Make the World a Better Place	41
An Honored Calling	47
The Power of One	53
Gifts of Value	59
Each New Day	65
Words of Praise	71
Remember That You're Needed	77
Small Daily Differences	83
Dare to Believe	89
You Are an Awakener	95
Unsung Heroes	101
Learn to Laugh	107
Classroom Management	113
A Passion for Knowledge	119
Learning for a Lifetime	125

God Made Teachers Special

You are not only my teacher. Rather, you are a friend, philosopher, and guide all molded into one person. I will always be grateful to you for your support.

On the sixth day, God created men and women. On the seventh day, He rested. Not so much to recuperate, but rather to prepare Himself for the work He was going to do on the next day. For it was on that day—the eighth day—that God created the first Teacher.

This Teacher, though taken from among men and women, had several significant modifications. In general, God made the Teacher more durable than other men and women. He made the Teacher tough...but gentle, too. Into the Teacher God poured a generous amount of patience. He gave the Teacher a heart slightly bigger than the average human heart. And He gave the Teacher an abundant supply of hope.

When God finished creating the Teacher, He stepped back and admired the work of His hands. And God saw that the Teacher was good. Very good! And God smiled, for when He looked at the Teacher, He saw into the future. He was placing the future in the hands of the Teacher.

And because God loves Teachers so much, on the ninth day God created "snow days."

I thank my God upon every remembrance of you.

PHILIPPIANS 1:3 NKJV

The measure of your real success
is one you cannot spend—
it's the way [a] child describes you
when talking to a friend.

MARTIN BUXBAUM

IT IS A SPECIAL *gift* TO BE ABLE

TO VIEW THE WORLD

THROUGH THE EYES OF A CHILD.

To love [a child] is to bring out the best in him, to teach
him to love what is difficult.

NADIA BOULANGER

The tender loving care of human beings
will never become obsolete.
People, even more than things, have to be
restored, renewed,
revived, reclaimed, and redeemed.
Never throw anybody out.

SAM LEVENSON

STAND OUTSIDE THIS EVENING.
LOOK AT THE *stars*. KNOW THAT
YOU ARE SPECIAL AND LOVED
BY THE ONE WHO CREATED THEM.

God made my life complete
when I placed all the pieces before Him....
God rewrote the text of my life
when I opened the book of my heart to His eyes.

PSALM 18:20, 24 THE MESSAGE

Teaching is sharing ourselves with others.
We get the best from our students when
we give the best of ourselves.

Before we even attempt to teach children, we want them
to know each of them is unique and very special.
We want them to like themselves, to want to achieve
and care about themselves.

MARVA COLLINS

Teaching is one of the few professions that permit love.

THEODORE ROETHKE

Some people are so special that once they enter your life,
it becomes richer and fuller and more wonderful
than you ever thought it could be.

Kids don't care what you think
until they think you care.

When my hands mold the clay of this child's life,
may the impressions be, in reality, made by
the movement of Your hands and directed
by Your perfect thoughts.
GLORIA GAITHER

Every child is shaped in and by the mind of God.

Lord, You are our Father.
We are the clay, and You are the potter.
We are all formed by Your hand.
ISAIAH 64:8 NLT

The Light of Understanding

My teacher, how can I ever thank you enough?
What you have given me will stay with me a lifetime.
Thank you for believing in me, for teaching me with
patience and understanding.

CATHERINE PULSIFER

Have you ever been at sea in a dense fog, when
it seemed as if a tangible white darkness shut you
in and the great ship, tense and anxious, groped
her way toward the shore with plummet and
sounding-line, and you waited with beating heart for
something to happen? I was like that ship before my
education began, only I was without compass or
sounding line, and no way of knowing how near the
harbor was. "Light! Give me light!" was the wordless cry
of my soul, and the light of love shone on me
in that very hour…. I have always thought it would be a
blessing if each person could be blind and deaf for a few
days during their early adult life. Darkness would make
them appreciate sight; silence would teach them
the joys of sound.

HELEN KELLER

For You will light my lamp;
The Lord my God will enlighten my darkness.
PSALM 18:28 NKJV

Every day we live is a priceless gift of God, loaded
with possibilities to learn something new,
to gain fresh insights.

DALE EVANS ROGERS

Your word is a lamp to guide my feet
and a light for my path.

PSALM 119:105 NLT

WHEN *teachers* LET THEIR LOVE
SHINE THROUGH, THEIR STUDENTS
ARE READY TO LEARN.

There is much satisfaction in work well done; praise is
sweet, but there can be no happiness equal to the joy of
finding a heart that understands.

VICTOR ROBINSON

Enthusiasm is the element of success in everything.
It is the light that leads and the strength that lifts
people on and up in the great struggles of scientific
pursuits and of professional labor.
It robs endurance of difficulty, and
makes duty a pleasure.

W. C. DOANE

MAY GOD GIVE YOU EYES
TO SEE *beauty* ONLY
THE HEART CAN UNDERSTAND.

Great teachers never strive to explain their vision.
They simply invite you to stand beside them
and see for yourself.

R. INMAN

O send out Your light and Your truth,
let them lead me.

PSALM 43:3 NASB

What other profession offers one the satisfaction
of knowing you have lit a spark in the mind of the
next generation and nurtured a fire that will burn
long after you've gone?

RAE ELLEN MCKEE

In my belief, you cannot deal with the
most serious things in the world unless you also
understand the most amusing.

SIR WINSTON CHURCHILL

O Lord above,
Give me work to do;
Give me health;
Give me joy in simple things.
Give me an eye for beauty,
A tongue for truth,
A heart that loves,
A mind that reasons,
A sympathy that understands;
Give me neither malice nor envy,
But a true kindness
And a noble common sense.
At the close of each day
Give me a book,
And a friend with whom
I can be silent.

Dreaming of Great Things

You are the molders of their dreams...the spark that
sets aflame the poet's hand or lights the flame
in some great singer's song.

CLARK MOLLENHOFF

Teaching is not a job, but a way of life. If you have
a zest for living, and are a cheerleader for life, then
the teaching profession is for you.... Being surrounded by
the enthusiasm of youth, you will be able to
continue to experience the wonders of learning
through your students' endeavors. Your creative juices
will know no bounds, and you will have the freedom
to allow your students to dream, as you
help guide them toward their dreams.

MARILYN BLACK

It is only by thinking about great and good
things that we come to love them,
and it is only by loving them
that we come to long for them,
and it is only by longing for them
that we are impelled to seek after them;
and it is only by seeking after them
that they become ours.

HENRY VAN DYKE

WHEN *dreams* COME TRUE AT LAST, THERE IS LIFE AND JOY.

PROVERBS 13:12 TLB

Let us think of education as the means of developing our greatest abilities, because in each of us there is a private hope and dream which, fulfilled, can be translated into benefit for everyone and greater strength for our nation.

JOHN F. KENNEDY

Far away, there in the sunshine, are my
highest aspirations. I may not reach them but
I can look up and see their beauty, believe in them,
and try to follow where they lead.

LOUISA MAY ALCOTT

We live in the present, we dream of the future, but we
learn eternal truths from the past.

LUCY MAUD MONTGOMERY

To dream anything that you want to dream:
that is the beauty of the human mind.
To do anything that you want to do:
that is the strength of the human will.
To trust yourself to test your limits:
that is the courage to succeed.

BERNARD EDMONDS

DO NOT *Pray* FOR DREAMS EQUAL
TO YOUR POWERS. *Pray* FOR POWERS
EQUAL TO YOUR DREAMS.

ADELAIDE ANN PROCTER

Commit yourself to a dream.... Nobody who tries to do
something great but fails is a total failure. Why?
Because they can always rest assured that they
succeeded in life's most important battle—
they defeated the fear of trying.

ROBERT SCHULLER

You are God! Your words are trustworthy,
and You have promised these good things.

2 SAMUEL 7:28 NIV

Most people think I am a dreamer.... We need visions
for larger things, for the unfolding and
reviewing of worthwhile things.

MARY MCLEOD BETHUNE

It's a thrill to fulfill your own childhood dreams, but
as you get older you may find that enabling the
dreams of others is even more fun.

RANDY PAUSCH

I came so they can have real and eternal life,
more and better life than they ever dreamed of.

JOHN 10:10 THE MESSAGE

It is necessary that we dream now and then. No one ever
achieved anything from the smallest to the greatest unless
the dream was dreamed first.

LAURA INGALLS WILDER

Only dreamers can teach us to soar.

ANNE MARIE PIERCE

Entrusted with the Future

Without you, I would have been lost. Thank you, teacher, for guiding me, inspiring me, and helping me become what I am today.

The future of the world is in my classroom today,
a future with the potential for good or bad....
Several future presidents are learning from me today;
so are the great writers of the next decades, and so
are all the so-called ordinary people who will make
the decisions in a democracy. I must never forget
these same young people could be the thieves and
murderers of the future. Only a teacher? Thank God
I have a calling to the greatest profession of all!
I must be vigilant every day, lest I lose one
fragile opportunity to improve tomorrow.

IVAN WELTON FITZWATER

How precious is Your lovingkindness, O God!
And the children of men take refuge
in the shadow of Your wings....
For with You is the fountain of life;
In Your light we see light.

PSALM 36:7, 9 NASB

Live for today but hold your hands open to tomorrow.
Anticipate the future and its changes with joy.
There is a seed of God's love in every event,
every circumstance, every unpleasant situation
in which you may find yourself.

BARBARA JOHNSON

EVENTS IN OUR *classrooms* TODAY

ARE THE SEEDS OF

WORLD EVENTS TOMORROW.

Lord...give me the gift of faith to be renewed and
shared with others each day. Teach me to live
this moment only, looking neither to the past
with regret, nor the future with apprehension.
Let love be my aim and my life a prayer.

ROSEANN ALEXANDER-ISHAM

Caring teachers are among our nation's greatest
treasures; they are entrusted with its future.

Neither the present nor the future,
nor any powers, neither height nor depth,
nor anything else in all creation,
will be able to separate us from the love of God.
ROMANS 8:38-39 NIV

I TOUCH THE *future*; I TEACH.

CHRISTA MCAULIFFE

Teachers, I believe, are the most responsible and
important members of society because their
professional efforts affect the fate of the earth.
HELEN CALDICOTT

Teaching children involves helping them shape their
ambitions and their sense of personal destiny.

GORDON MACDONALD

A student's future is built upon the foundation of the
lessons taught by a few outstanding teachers.

Every material goal, even if it is met, will pass away.
But the heritage of children is timeless.
Our children are our messages to the future.

BILLY GRAHAM

"For I know the plans I have for you,"
declares the Lord, "plans to prosper you and
not to harm you, plans to give you hope and a future."

JEREMIAH 29:11 NIV

I'll show my children right from wrong,
encourage dreams and hope;
explain respect for others,
while teaching them to cope
with outside pressures, inside fears,
a world that's less than whole;
and through it all I'll nurture
my children's most precious soul!
Though oftentimes a struggle,
this job I'll never trade;
for in my hand tomorrow lives…
a future God has made.

In every child is planted the seed
of a great future.

Press On

The world will always need teachers like you—
so understanding, so helpful, so caring.
Thanks for not giving up on me!

Nothing in the world can take the place of persistence.
Talent will not; nothing is more common than
unsuccessful men with talent. Genius will not;
unrewarded genius is almost a proverb. Education
will not; the world is full of educated derelicts.
Persistence and determination are omnipotent.
The slogan "press on" has solved and always will
solve the problems of the human race. No person
was ever honored for what he received. Honor
has been the reward for what he gave.

CALVIN COOLIDGE

I pray that your love for each other will overflow
more and more, and that you will keep on growing
in your knowledge and understanding.

PHILIPPIANS 1:9 NLT

Teachers teach because they care. Teaching
young people is what they do best. It requires
long hours, patience, and care.

HORACE MANN

If your determination is fixed, I do not counsel you
to despair. Few things are impossible to
diligence and skill. Great works are performed
not by strength, but perseverance.

SAMUEL JOHNSON

Persistent people begin their
success where others
end in failure.

EDWARD EGGLESTON

There are four steps to accomplishment:
Plan Purposefully.
Prepare Prayerfully.
Proceed Positively.
Pursue Persistently.

Success is failure turned inside out,
The silver tint of the clouds of doubt,
And you never can tell how close you are,
It may be near when it seems so far.
So stick to the fight when you're hardest hit,
It's when things seem worst,
That you must not quit.

I CAN DO ALL THINGS THROUGH *Christ* WHO STRENGTHENS ME.

PHILIPPIANS 4:13 NKJV

There are no limits to our opportunities. Most of us
see only a small portion of what is possible.
We create opportunities by seeing the possibilities
and having the persistence to act upon them. We must
always remember...opportunities are always here,
but we must look for them.

PRESS ON

. . . .

In teaching you cannot see the fruit of a day's work. It is
invisible and remains so, maybe for twenty years.

JACQUES BARZUN

You climb a long ladder until you can see over the roof,
or over the clouds.... You watch your shod feet step on
each round rung, one at a time; you do not hurry and do
not rest.... You climb steadily, doing your job in the dark.
When you reach the end, there is nothing more to climb.
The sun hits you. The bright wideness surprises you;
you had forgotten there was an end. You look back at the
ladder's two feet on the distant grass, astonished.

ANNIE DILLARD

We are continually faced by great opportunities
brilliantly disguised as insoluble problems.

33

'Tis a lesson you should heed,
Try, try again;
If at first you don't succeed,
Try, try again;
Then your courage should appear,
For, if you will persevere,
You will conquer, never fear;
Try, try again.

W. E. HICKSON

Life's great opportunities often open
on the road of daily duties.

Keep on sowing your seed, for you never know
which will grow—perhaps it all will.

ECCLESIASTES 11:6 TLB

A Work of Heart

If I were to make a solemn speech in praise of you,
in gratitude, in deep affection, you would turn
an alarming shade of crimson and try to escape.
So I won't. Take it all as said.

Marion C. Garretty

The attitudes of teachers and students have the
greatest influence on learning.... Inspiring students
with a sense of their own worth gives them the
confidence to express themselves more freely,
to explore and learn through their mistakes,
and to regard learning as an adventure....
The teacher's kind disposition, aside from being
a good educational tool, has an importance
beyond the mere teaching of subject matter.
The demonstration of love, understanding,
and forgiveness is a human lesson profoundly
vital to the education of each pupil in growth
toward maturity and humanity.

JAY SOMMER

All of you should be of one mind. Sympathize with each
other. Love each other as brothers and sisters.
Be tenderhearted, and keep a humble attitude.

1 PETER 3:8 NLT

THE BEST TEACHERS TEACH FROM THE *heart*, NOT FROM THE BOOK.

CAROL JOHNSTON

The essence of teaching is to make learning contagious,
to have one idea spark another.

MARVA COLLINS

It is not the job that determines its worth and impact,
rather the heart of the person approaching and executing
the task. No work in itself is spiritual or secular.

JEAN FLEMING

When I approach a child, he inspires in me
two sentiments: tenderness for what he is, and
respect for what he may become.

LOUIS PASTEUR

Love is patient, love is kind...; bears all things,
believes all things, hopes all things, endures all things.
Love never fails.

1 Corinthians 13:4, 7-8 nasb

Each one of us is God's special work of art.
Through us, He teaches and inspires,
delights and encourages, informs and uplifts
all those who view our lives....
A painting like no other in all of time.

Joni Eareckson Tada

Far and away the best prize that *life* offers is the chance to work hard at work worth doing.

Theodore Roosevelt

To reach a child's mind a teacher must capture his heart.
Only if a child feels right can he think right.

HAIM G. GINOTT

You can never go home without a smile on your
face when you teach kids. I was always beaming
at the end of the day. And it was so inspirational
each morning to see that the kids were excited to be
back at school.... I still cannot get used to how much
my heart soars with every student's success,
and how a piece of my heart is plucked away
when any student slips away.

DELISSA L. MAI

O dearest [child], My heart for better lore
would seldom yearn,
could I but teach the hundredth part of what
from thee I learn.

William Wordsworth

Now he who plants and he who waters are one,
and each one will receive his own reward
according to his own labor.

1 Corinthians 3:8 nkjv

One should take children's philosophy to heart.
They do not despise a bubble because it bursts.
They immediately set to work
to blow another one.

*To Make
the World a
Better Place*

You've made me a better person. Wherever I may go in
my life, I will always remember that I had an excellent
guide in the form of a teacher: You!

The price of success is hard work, dedication to the job at hand, and the determination that whether we win or lose, we have applied the best of ourselves to the task at hand.... The quality of a person's life is in direct proportion to their commitment to excellence, regardless of their chosen field of endeavor.

VINCENT T. LOMBARDI

Let us not lose heart in doing good, for in due time we will reap if we do not grow weary. So then, while we have opportunity, let us do good to all people.

GALATIANS 6:9-10 NASB

THE SMALLEST GOOD *deed* IS BETTER THAN THE GRANDEST INTENTION.

The task of the excellent teacher is to stimulate "apparently ordinary" people to unusual effort. The tough problem is not in identifying winners: it is in making winners out of ordinary people.

K. PATRICIA CROSS

There is a latent desire in every human being to do something of worth that will have lasting significance... something that will make life better for others.

TONY CAMPOLO

Whoever first coined the phrase "you're the wind beneath my wings" most assuredly was reflecting on the sublime influence of a very special teacher.

FRANK TRUJILLO

There is no medicine like hope, no incentive
so great, and no tonic so powerful as
expectation of something better tomorrow.

Whatever things are true, whatever things are noble,
whatever things are just, whatever things are pure,
whatever things are lovely, whatever things are of good
report, if there is any virtue, and if there is anything
praiseworthy—meditate on these things.

PHILIPPIANS 4:8 NKJV

The highest excellence which an individual can attain
must be to work according to the best of his genius and to
work in harmony with God's creation.

J. H. SMYTH

One hundred years from now it will not matter
what kind of car I drove, what kind of house I lived in,
or how much money I had in the bank.
One hundred years from now it will not matter
what kind of computer I used, what kind of school
I attended, or how many degrees I had.
But the world will be a little better,
because I was important in the life of a child.

THERE IS NO BETTER EXERCISE FOR THE HEART THAN REACHING DOWN AND *lifting* PEOPLE UP.

JOHN ANDREW HOLMER

Do what you can to show you care about other people,
and you will make our world a better place.

ROSALYNN CARTER

Teach us to number our days,
That we may present to You a heart of wisdom.

PSALM 90:12 NASB

Open your eyes, your ears, your mind, your heart,
your spirit and you'll find adventure everywhere....
It is in your daily work, whether you are
keeping books, making sales, teaching school,
building bridges, driving a truck....
Think of whatever you are doing as an adventure
and watch your life change for the better.

WILFERD A. PETERSON

An Honored Calling

I think of you not only as a teacher, but as a role model,
mentor, leader, guide, and friend. Thank you for
being all those things and more.

What constitutes success?
They have achieved success who have lived well;
laughed often and loved much;
who have gained the respect of intelligent people
and the love of little children;
who have filled their niche and accomplished their task;
who have left the world better than they found it,
whether by an improved poppy,
a perfect poem or a rescued soul;
who have never lacked appreciation of
earth's beauty, or failed to express it;
who have always looked for the best in others
and given the best they had;
whose life was an inspiration;
whose memory a benediction.

BESSIE ANDERSON STANLEY

To this you were called
so that you may inherit a blessing.

I PETER 3:9 NIV

Teaching is a calling, not a choice.

MARY ANN ALEXANDER

There's no word in the language I revere more than
"teacher." My heart sings when a kid refers to me as his
teacher, and it always has. I've honored myself and the
entire family of man by becoming a teacher.

PAT CONROY

DEDICATE *yourself* TO THE CALL

OF YOUR HEART AND

SEE WHERE IT LEADS YOU.

Remember that your work comes only moment
by moment, and as surely as God calls you to work,
He gives the strength to do it.

PRISCILLA MAURICE

I pray also that the eyes of your heart may be
enlightened in order that you may know
the hope to which He has called you.

EPHESIANS 1:18 NIV

WE ARE NOT *called* BY GOD
TO EXTRAORDINARY THINGS,
BUT TO DO ORDINARY THINGS
WITH EXTRAORDINARY LOVE.

JEAN VANIER

It is my calling to treat every human being with
grace and dignity, to treat every person, whether
encountered in a palace or a gas station, as a life
made in the image of God.

SHEILA WALSH

Your job is to teach them the rules and instructions,
to show them how to live, what to do.
EXODUS 18:20 THE MESSAGE

The important thing really is not the deed
well done or the medal that you possess,
but the dedication and dreams
out of which they grow.
ROBERT H. BENSON

In a perfectly rational society, the best of us would aspire
to be teachers and the rest of us would have to settle for
something less, because passing civilization along from
one generation to the next ought to be the highest honor
and highest responsibility anyone could have.
LEE IACOCCA

We find our greatest joy, not in getting, but
in expressing what we are. We do not really live
for honors or for pay; our gladness is not in the
taking and holding, but in the doing, the striving,
the building, the living. It is a higher joy to teach
than to be taught.... The happy person is the one who
lives the life of love, not for the honors it may bring,
but for the life itself.

R. J. BAUGHAN

There is no greater pleasure than bringing to the
uncluttered, supple mind of a child the delight
of knowing God and the many rich things
He has given us to enjoy.

GLADYS M. HUNT

The
Power of
One

None of my other teachers held me up to the same
standard as my English teacher.... I eventually learned
to hold myself up to the same standard.

MELISSA MACOMBER

There is not enough darkness in all the world
to put out the light of one small candle....
In moments of discouragement, defeat, or even
despair, there are always certain things to cling to.
Little things usually: remembered laughter,
the face of a sleeping child, a tree in the wind—
in fact, any reminder of something deeply felt
or dearly loved. No man is so poor
as not to have many of these small candles.
When they are lighted, darkness goes away
and a touch of wonder remains.

SIR ARTHUR GORDON

THE ONE WHO *blesses* OTHERS
IS ABUNDANTLY BLESSED; THOSE WHO
HELP OTHERS ARE HELPED.

PROVERBS 11:25 THE MESSAGE

Live your life while you have it.
Life is a splendid gift—
there is nothing small about it.

FLORENCE NIGHTINGALE

No pessimist ever discovered the secrets of the stars,
or sailed to an uncharted land, or opened
a new heaven to the human spirit.

HELEN KELLER

One taper lights a thousand,
Yet shines as it has shone;
And the humblest light may kindle
One brighter than its own.

HEZEKIAH BUTTERWORTH

A span of life is nothing. But the man or woman
who lives that span, they are something.
They can fill that tiny span with meaning,
so its quality is immeasurable, though
its quantity may be insignificant.

CHAIM POTOK

Let us think of ways to motivate one another
to acts of love and good works.

HEBREWS 10:24 NLT

When you grow up in an environment where…
commitment and dedication is not just talked about
but lived so fully, so honestly, there is no way
that it does not take root in your being.

YOLANDA KING

"Of all who live, I am the one by whom
This work can best be done in the right way."
Then shall I see it not too great, nor small,
To suit my spirit; and to prove my power;
Then shall I cheerful greet the laboring hours,
And cheerful turn when the long shadows fall
At eventide, to play and love and rest,
Because I know for me my work is best.

HENRY VAN DYKE

EACH OF US HAS SOMETHING
DIFFERENT TO *contribute*, AND
NO MATTER HOW SMALL OR
INSIGNIFICANT IT MAY SEEM,
IT CAN BE FOR THE BENEFIT OF ALL.

LAURITZ MELCHIOR

You have a unique message to deliver,
a unique song to sing, a unique act of love
to bestow. This message, this song,
and this act of love have been entrusted
exclusively to the one and only you.

JOHN POWELL

What happens when we live God's way?
He brings gifts into our lives, much the same way
that fruit appears in an orchard—things like
affection for others, exuberance about life, serenity.
We develop a willingness to stick with things,
a sense of compassion in the heart.

GALATIANS 5:22-23 THE MESSAGE

Gifts of Value

Through the time I have spent with you,
you have given me one of the most valuable gifts:
the power to see my true potential.

Shaelee Barker

I teach little children to read. I hold the values of our culture and the history of our world before them like a sweet confection.... I possess the power to lace their intake with arsenic or sweet nectar, creating their self-esteem or destroying it. I shudder under the burden of such a responsibility.... However, where it is always appropriate to hold teachers accountable for doing their job, which is teaching, it is not always possible to hold them responsible for doing the student's job, which is learning.

RAE ELLEN MCKEE

TENDING TO THE WEAKEST AMONG US *teaches* US THE POWER OF TRUE STRENGTH.

CHRISTOPHER DE VINCK

Only a child can see any value
in rain puddles.

My grace is sufficient for you, for My strength
is made perfect in weakness.

2 CORINTHIANS 12:9 NKJV

It is not the work we do that is so important. It's the
people we work with. It's the work God does in our lives
through them. And it's the work He does in their lives
through us. That is what's sacred.

KEN GIRE

How do I love God?... By doing beautifully the work I
have been given to do, by doing simply that which God
has entrusted to me, in whatever form it may take.

MOTHER TERESA

Priceless in value, we are handcrafted
by God, who has a personal design
and plan for each of us.

Are not five sparrows sold for two copper coins?
And not one of them is forgotten before God.
But the very hairs of your head are all numbered.
Do not fear therefore; you are of more
value than many sparrows.

LUKE 12:6-7 NKJV

There's no thrill in easy sailing
when the skies are clear and blue,
There's no joy in merely doing things
which any one can do.
But there is some satisfaction
that is mighty sweet to take,
when you reach a destination
that you thought you'd never make.

It is my belief that God gives us all gifts, special
abilities that we have the privilege of developing
to help us serve Him and humanity.

BENJAMIN CARSON

NEVER UNDERESTIMATE
THE *influence*
OF A CARING TEACHER.

I determined that there should not be a minute in the day
when my children should not be aware by my face and my
lips that my heart was theirs, that their happiness was my
happiness and their pleasures my pleasures.

JOHANN HEINRICH PESTALOZZI

Loving teachers will allow
time and indulgence while a child grows,
experiments, and plays.

Be kind to one another, tenderhearted,
forgiving one another.

Ephesians 4:32 NKJV

Once we discover how to appreciate
the timeless values in our daily experiences,
we can enjoy the best things in life.

Teach me, Father, to value each day, to live,
to love, to laugh, to play.

Kathy Mills

Each
New Day

At the end of each day, she would tell the class, "Remember, tomorrow is a new day. If you've made mistakes today, you can have a fresh start." I think she would be surprised to know how powerfully that thought has affected my life.

God give me joy in the common things:
In the dawn that lures, the eve that sings.
In the new grass sparkling after rain,
In the late wind's wild and weird refrain;
In the springtime's spacious field of gold,
In the precious light by winter doled....
In the songs of children, unrestrained;
In the sober wisdom age has gained.
God give me joy in the tasks that press,
In the memories that burn and bless;
In the thought that life has love to spend,
In the faith that God's at journey's end.

THOMAS CURTIS CLARK

This is the day the Lord has made;
We will rejoice and be glad in it.

PSALM 118:24 NKJV

Face the work of every day with the influence of a few
thoughtful, quiet moments with your heart and God.
L. B. COWMAN

Today is unique! It has never occurred before
and it will never be repeated. At midnight
it will end, quietly, suddenly, totally. Forever.
But the hours between now and then are
opportunities with eternal possibilities.
CHARLES R. SWINDOLL

EACH OF MY *days* ARE MIRACLES.
I WON'T WASTE MY DAY;
I WON'T THROW AWAY A MIRACLE.

KELLEY VICKSTROM

Service is the rent we each pay for living.
It is not something to do in your spare time;
it is the very purpose of life.

MARIAN WRIGHT EDELMAN

ALL THE DAYS ORDAINED FOR ME
WERE *written* IN YOUR BOOK
BEFORE ONE OF THEM CAME TO BE.

PSALM 139:16 NIV

No other job offers you the opportunity to be in control
of your own daily plan, and to work in an environment
where every day is different. Because you will be working
with youth, routine is non-existent and each day will
present new challenges.

MARILYN BLACK

Better than a thousand days of diligent study is
one day with a great teacher.

JAPANESE PROVERB

This bright, new day, complete with 24 hours of
opportunities, choices, and attitudes comes with a
perfectly matched set of 1,440 minutes. This unique gift,
this one day, cannot be exchanged, replaced or refunded.
Handle with care. Make the most of it. There is
only one to a customer!

Show me Your ways, O Lord,
teach me Your paths;
guide me in Your truth and teach me,
for You are God my Savior,
and my hope is in You all day long.

PSALM 25:4-5 NIV

Life is a coin. You can spend it any way you wish,
but you can spend it only once.

LILLIAN DICKSON

All the absurd little meetings, decisions, and
skirmishes that go to make up our days. It all
adds up to very little, and yet it all adds up
to very much. Our days are full of nonsense,
and yet not, because it is precisely into the
nonsense of our days that God speaks to us
words of great significance.

FREDERICK BUECHNER

Words of Praise

Thanks for the push when I needed it and for the encouragement to try every day.

Encouragement is awesome. It has the capacity
to lift a man's or woman's shoulders. To spark
the flicker of a smile on the face of a discouraged child.
To breathe fresh fire into the fading embers
of a smoldering dream. To actually change the
course of another human being's day, week, or life.
CHARLES R. SWINDOLL

A WORD OF PRAISE IS A "VERBAL TROPHY," AND EVERY CHILD HAS *abundant* SHELF SPACE FOR SUCH HONORS.

JAN DARGATZ

Be patient with each person, attentive to individual
needs.... Look for the best in each other, and
always do your best to bring it out.
I THESSALONIANS 5:14-15 THE MESSAGE

I try to make it possible for all my students to have a chance to be successful at tasks that suit their talents and to see that someone loves them and cares about what they accomplish. I personally invite all my students to become active participants in their own learning.

BRUCE E. BROMBACHER

Affection is the most satisfying reward a child can receive. It costs nothing, is readily available, and provides great encouragement.

I'll show these children right from wrong,
encourage dreams and hope;
explain respect for others,
while teaching them to cope
with outside pressures, inside fears,
a world that's less than whole;
and through it all I'll nurture
each child's most precious soul!
Though oftentimes a struggle,
this job I'll never trade;
for in my hand tomorrow lives…
a future God has made.

Let me be a little kinder,
Let me be a little blinder
To the faults of those about me;
Let me praise a little more.
Let me be, when I am weary,
Just a little bit more cheery;
Let me serve a little better
Those that I am striving for.

Let me be a little braver
When temptation bids me waver;
Let me strive a little harder
To be all that I should be.
Let me be a little meeker
With my brother who is weeker;
Let me think more of my neighbor
And a little less of me.

May God who gives patience, steadiness, and
encouragement help you to live in
complete harmony with each other.

ROMANS 15:5 TLB

. . . .

There are times when encouragement means such a lot.
And a word is enough to convey it.
GRACE STRICKER DAWSON

People have a way of
becoming what you
encourage them to be.

SCUDDER N. PARKER

When we really love others, we accept them as they are.
We make our love visible through little acts of kindness,
shared activities, words of praise and thanks, and our
willingness to get along with them.
EDWARD E. FORD

A student never forgets an encouraging private word,
when it is given with sincere respect and admiration.
WILLIAM LYON PHELPS

Like apples of gold in settings of silver
Is a word spoken in right circumstances.
Like an earring of gold and an ornament of fine gold
Is a wise reprover to a listening ear.

PROVERBS 25:11-12 NASB

Children are like wet cement. Whatever falls on them
makes an impression.

HAIM GINOTT

Encouragement is being a good listener, being positive,
letting others know you accept them for who they are.
It is offering hope, caring about the feelings of another,
understanding.

GIGI GRAHAM TCHIVIDJIAN

Praise does wonders for our sense of hearing.

ARNOLD H. GLASGOW

Remember That You're Needed

You're a foundation builder....
What could be more important than helping
to shape and mold others' lives?

GUY RICE DOUD

With a special gift for learning
And with a heart that deeply cares,
You add a lot of love
To everything you share.
And even though you mean a lot,
You'll never know how much,
For you helped to change the world
Through every life you touched.
You sparked the creativity
In the students whom you taught
And helped them to strive for goals,
For dreams that can't be bought.
You are such a special teacher
That no words can truly tell
How very much you're valued
For the work you do so well.

And let the loveliness of our Lord, our God, rest on us,
confirming the work that we do.

PSALM 90:17 THE MESSAGE

Remember, if you ever need a helping hand,
you'll find one at the end of your arm.
As you grow older, you will discover
that you have two hands,
one for helping yourself,
the other for helping others.
SAM LEVENSON

Be humble and gentle. Be patient with each other, making
allowance for each other's faults because of your love.
EPHESIANS 4:2 TLB

MOST *children* NEED MORE LOVE THAN THEY DESERVE.

Attaching high value to a child means being attentive and
responsive to that child's needs.
GARY SMALLEY & JOHN TRENT

What is important is not what you do as a teacher, but what your students learn as a result of what you do.

HOWARD HENDRICKS

If a child is to keep his inborn sense of wonder...
he needs the companionship of at least
one adult who can share it, rediscovering
with him the joy, excitement, and mystery
of the world we live in.

RACHEL CARSON

THE MOST IMPORTANT
educational EXPERIENCE

HAPPENING TO STUDENTS

IS THEIR TEACHER.

VIRGIL E. HERRICK

Just as there are no little people or unimportant lives,
there is no insignificant work.

ELENA BONNER

Upon the subject of education, not presuming
to dictate any plan or system respecting it, I can
only say that I view it as the most important subject
which we as a people may be engaged in. That everyone
may receive at least a moderate education appears to be
an objective of vital importance.

ABRAHAM LINCOLN

To enjoy your work...is indeed a gift from God.
The person who does that will not need to look back with
sorrow on his past, for God gives him joy.

ECCLESIASTES 5:20 TLB

Half the joy of life is in little things taken on the run.
Let us run if we must—even the sands do that—but let us
keep our hearts young and our eyes open that nothing
worth our while shall escape us. And everything is worth
its while if we only grasp it and its significance.

VICTOR CHERBULIEZ

Remember that you are needed. There is
at least one important work to be done
that will not be done unless you do it.

CHARLES L. ALLEN

Small Daily Differences

My teacher thought I was smarter than I was; so I was.

SIX-YEAR-OLD STUDENT

When you thought I wasn't looking,
you gave me a sticker,
and I knew that little things were special things.
When you thought I wasn't looking,
you put your arm around me,
and I felt loved.

When you thought I wasn't looking,
I saw tears come from your eyes,
and I learned that sometimes things hurt—
but that it's alright to cry....
When you thought I wasn't looking, you cared,
and I wanted to be everything I could be.
When you thought I wasn't looking—I looked...and
Wanted to say Thanks for all those things you did
when you thought I wasn't looking.

MARY RITA SCHILKE KORZAN

We must not, in trying to think about how we can make
a big difference, ignore the small daily differences
we can make which, over time, add up to big
differences that we often cannot foresee.

Marian Wright Edelman

WORK *willingly* AT WHATEVER

YOU DO, AS THOUGH YOU WERE

WORKING FOR THE LORD

RATHER THAN FOR PEOPLE.

COLOSSIANS 3:23 NLT

A child, unlike any other, yet identical to all those who
have preceded and all who will follow, sits in a classroom
today—hopeful, enthusiastic, curious. The touch of a
teacher will make the difference!

SHARON M. DRAPER

God, Your heart is the most sensitive and tender
of all. No act goes unnoticed, no matter
how insignificant or small....
Thank You for paying attention to small things.
Thank You for valuing the insignificant....
Thank You far caring about me.

RICHARD J. FOSTER

YOU BECOME GREAT BY ACCEPTING,
NOT ASSERTING. YOUR *spirit*, NOT
YOUR SIZE, MAKES THE DIFFERENCE.

LUKE 9:48 THE MESSAGE

Whoever welcomes a little child like this in My name
welcomes Me.

MATTHEW 18:5 NIV

Choices can change our lives profoundly. The choice to
mend a broken relationship, to say "yes" to a difficult
assignment, to lay aside some important work to play
with a child, to visit some forgotten person—these small
choices may affect many lives eternally.

GLORIA GAITHER

God has a history of using the insignificant
to accomplish the impossible.

RICHARD EXLEY

Whether we are poets or parents or teachers or
artists or gardeners, we must start where we are
and use what we have. In the process of creation and
relationship, what seems mundane and trivial may show
itself to be holy, precious, part of a pattern.

LUCI SHAW

Thank you, God, for little things
That often come our way,
The things we take for granted
But don't mention when we pray.

The unexpected courtesy,
The thoughtful kindly deed,
A hand reached out to help us
In the time of sudden need.

Oh, make us more aware, dear God,
Of little daily graces
That come to us with sweet surprise
From never-dreamed-of places.

Dare to Believe

You have a special way of caring and
bringing out the best in all your students.
Thanks for daring to believe the best of us.

Only the brave should teach.
Only those who love the young should teach.
Teaching is a vocation.
It is as sacred as the priesthood;
as innate as a desire,
as inescapable as the genius which compels a great artist.
If one has not the concern for humanity,
the love of living creatures,
the vision of the priest and the artist,
one must not teach.

PEARL S. BUCK

Teaching is an exhausting job. I did not, however,
expect to be emotionally exhausted. I suppose
the easiest way out of this dilemma would be
to make myself emotionally unavailable
to my students.... Not this teacher.
This teacher can't help but share in some of
those emotional moments. I can't turn off a
portion of myself when I walk into the classroom.
It's either all of me or nothing.

ALLISON L. BAER

The work in front of you is God's work and not yours.
If God wants it to succeed, it will. If God doesn't,
it won't. What God wants of you is to try!
So have courage—and move.

IGNATIUS OF LOYOLA

THERE IS NO FEAR IN LOVE;
BUT *perfect* LOVE CASTS OUT FEAR.

1 JOHN 4:18 NKJV

God is a safe place to hide,
ready to help when we need Him.
We stand fearless at the cliff-edge of doom,
courageous in seastorm and earthquake.

PSALM 46:1-2 THE MESSAGE

YOU CANNOT TEACH OTHERS ANYTHING. YOU CAN ONLY HELP THEM TO *discover* IT WITHIN THEMSELVES.

GALILEO GALILEI

To learn is to change. Education is a process
that changes the learner.
GEORGE B. LEONARD

Make no little plans; they have no magic to stir [the soul]
and probably themselves will not be realized. Make big
plans; aim high in hope and work, remembering that a
noble, logical diagram once recorded will not die.
DANIEL H. BURNHAM

Don't be afraid to give your best to what seemingly are small jobs. Every time you conquer one it makes you that much stronger. If you do the little jobs well, the big ones will tend to take care of themselves.

DALE CARNEGIE

Do not fear, for I am with you;
Do not anxiously look about you, for I am your God.
I will strengthen you, surely I will help you,
Surely I will uphold you with My righteous right hand.

ISAIAH 41:10 NASB

Dare to love and to be a real friend. The love you give and receive is a reality that will lead you closer and closer to God as well as to those whom God has given you to love.

HENRI J. M. NOUWEN

God, grant me wisdom,
Grant me vision,
Grant me courage,
Grant me love,
To teach a child.

IDA NELLE HOLLAWAY

I would be true, for there are those who trust me;
I would be pure, for there are those who care;
I would be strong, for there is much to suffer;
I would be brave, for there is much to dare.

I would be of all—the foe, the friendless;
I would be giving, and forget the gift;
I would be humble, for I know my weakness;
I would look up, and laugh, and love, and lift.

HOWARD ARNOLD WALTER

You Are an Awakener

My teacher gave me the gift of a place
where no question was a stupid question,
a safe haven of curiosity and exploration and discovery.

My first precept about teaching is to accept
every child entrusted to me because each one
is his parents' greatest gift. It is my job to accept him
as he is, teach him what I must, and help him reach
a new and better understanding of himself and
the world in which he lives.... Teaching is a timeless
profession. It is the basis of all other professions.
Good teachers plant the seeds that make good doctors,
good accountants, good public servants, good statesmen,
good taxi drivers and good astronauts.

MARY V. BICOUVARIS

God is able to make all grace abound to you, so that
in all things at all times, having all that you need,
you will abound in every good work.

2 CORINTHIANS 9:8 NIV

WHATEVER YOU DO,

PUT ROMANCE AND ENTHUSIASM
INTO THE *lives* OF OUR CHILDREN.

MARGARET R. MACDONALD

I studied the lives of great men and famous women, and
I found that the men and women who got to the top were
those who did the jobs they had in hand with everything
they had of energy and enthusiasm and hard work.

HARRY S. TRUMAN

Life begets life. Energy creates energy.
It is by spending oneself that one becomes rich.

SARAH BERNHARDT

I am not a teacher...I am an awakener.

ROBERT FROST

I don't dream of wealth and success for you.
But instead, a job you like, skills you can perfect,
enthusiasm to lighten your heart, friends,
and love in abundance.

PAM BROWN

A CHILD IS...AN *island*

OF CURIOSITY SURROUNDED

BY A SEA OF QUESTION MARKS.

Don't you see that children are God's best gift?...
His generous legacy?

PSALM 127:3 THE MESSAGE

The art of the creative teacher is to awaken the natural
curiosity of eager young minds.

The huge dome of the sky is of all things
sensuously perceived the most like infinity.
When God made space and worlds that move in space,
and clothed our world with air, and gave us such eyes
and such imaginations as those we have, He knew
what the sky would mean to us…. We cannot be
certain that this was not indeed one of the
chief purposes for which Nature was created.
C. S. Lewis

We need to recapture the power of imagination;
we shall find that life can be full of
wonder, mystery, beauty, and joy.
Sir Harold Spencer Jones

Enthusiasm is a kind of faith that has been set on fire.

GEORGE MATTHEW ADAMS

God has given each of us the ability to do
certain things well. So...if you are a teacher,
do a good job of teaching.

ROMANS 12:6-7 TLB

The imagination should be allowed a certain amount of
time to browse around.

THOMAS MERTON

A young child, a fresh, uncluttered mind,
a world before him—to what treasures
will you lead him?

GLADYS M. HUNT

Unsung Heroes

You're my hero! I will always be thankful to you,
my teacher, for all the hard work and effort
you have invested in my education.

Thanks FOR...

making the difference

long, long hours

creating a sense of family

being the keeper of dreams

using good judgment

teaching for learning

making reading fun

forgiving

being the wind beneath my wings

that sensitive touch

never giving up on anybody

believing in miracles

respecting each other

taking responsibility for all students

keeping a tight rein on discipline

striving for excellence, not perfection

being brave

smiling a lot

never depriving our children of hope

being tough minded but tender hearted
showing enthusiasm even when you don't feel like it
keeping your promises
giving your best
your wisdom and courage
being punctual and insisting on it in others
providing creative solutions
avoiding the negative and seeking out the good
being there when students need you
listening
doing more than is expected
never giving up on what you really want
remaining open, flexible, and curious
being a friend
sharing
keeping several irons in the fire
being a child's hero
going the distance
having a good sense of humor
being a dream maker
giving your heart.

Do not neglect doing good and sharing,
for with such sacrifices God is pleased.
HEBREWS 13:16 NASB

In our world of big names, curiously our true heroes
tend to be anonymous. In this life of illusion and
quasi-illusion, the person of solid virtues who can be
admired for something more substantial than
his well-knownness often proves to be the unsung hero:
the teacher, the nurse, the mother, the honest cop,
the hard worker at lonely, underpaid,
unglamorous, unpublicized jobs.
DANIEL J. BOORSTIN

Nurture your mind with great thoughts;
to believe in the heroic makes heroes.
BENJAMIN DISRAELI

God has given each of you some special abilities; be sure
to use them to help each other, passing on to others
God's many kinds of blessings.

1 PETER 4:10 TLB

A LITTLE THING IS A LITTLE THING, BUT *faithfulness* IN A LITTLE THING IS A BIG THING.

HUDSON TAYLOR

I long to accomplish a great and noble task, but
it is my chief duty to accomplish humble tasks
as though they were great and noble. The world
is moved along, not only by the mighty shoves
of its heroes, but also by the aggregate of the
tiny pushes of each honest worker.

HELEN KELLER

Going far beyond the call of duty, doing more
than others expect...is what excellence is all about.
And it comes from striving, maintaining the highest
standards, looking after the smallest detail,
and going the extra mile. Excellence means
doing your very best. In everything. In every way.

Anyone who welcomes a little child like this on My behalf
welcomes Me, and anyone who welcomes Me
welcomes...My Father who sent Me.

MARK 9:37 NLT

Learn to Laugh

Often, when I am reading a good book, I stop
and thank my teacher. That is, I used to,
until she got an unlisted number.

We were doing a science lesson on how plants grow.
The children all got a chance to plant their own seeds.
As the teacher, I planted a few extra seeds for the
children whose plants might not sprout. After a few
weeks of watching them, I secretly exchanged a few.
The next day one of my students said,
"Look, Teacher. It's a miracle! My plant is growing."
I said, "Yes, seeds sprouting is very exciting."
He said, "No, Teacher, that's not the miracle.
I *ate* the *seed* and it's growing anyway!"

DEBBIE CAPUANO

A merry heart does good, like medicine.

PROVERBS 17:22 NKJV

If you can learn to laugh in spite of the circumstances that
surround you, you will enrich others, enrich yourself, and
more than that, you will last!

BARBARA JOHNSON

IT NOW COSTS MORE TO *amuse* A
CHILD THAN IT ONCE DID
TO EDUCATE HIS FATHER.

H. V. PROCHNOW

The real joy of life is in its play. Play is anything we do
for the joy and love of doing it, apart from any profit,
compulsion, or sense of duty. It is the real living of life
with the feeling of freedom and self-expression.
Play is the business of childhood, and its continuation
in later years is the prolongation of youth.

WALTER RAUSCHENBUSCH

Let all who take refuge in You be glad,
Let them ever sing for joy.

PSALM 5:11 NASB

A keen sense of humor helps us to overlook the
unbecoming, understand the unconventional, tolerate
the unpleasant, over come the unexpected, and
outlast the unbearable.

BILLY GRAHAM

YOU KNOW CHILDREN ARE GROWING
UP WHEN THEY START *asking*
QUESTIONS THAT HAVE ANSWERS.

J. J. PLOMP

Laughter dulls the sharpest pain and flattens out
the greatest stress. To share it is to give a gift
of health because, as someone pointed out,
"Ulcers can't grow while you're laughing."

HUNTER "PATCH" ADAMS

Teachers have to:
stand above all their students, yet be on their level;
be able to do 180 other things not connected
with the subject they teach;
run on coffee, Cokes, and leftovers;
communicate vital knowledge to thousands
of students daily and be right;
have as much, and sometimes more, time
for the job as they do for themselves;
and have a smile that can endure everything
from practical jokes to referendum votes.
Teachers are an absolute miracle.

Children are unpredictable.
You never know what inconsistency
they're going to catch you in next.
FRANKLIN P. JONES

The joy of the Lord is your strength.

NEHEMIAH 8:10 TLB

Laugh at yourself. You will always be
your greatest source of humor. Don't ever
take yourself so seriously that you can't find
humor in the things you say and do.

BRUCE BICKLE AND STAN JANTZ

When the going gets tough,
the tough take a coffee break.

Classroom Management

We think of the effective teachers we have had over the years with a sense of recognition, but those who have touched our humanity we remember with a deep sense of gratitude.

A school teacher injured his back and had to
wear a plaster cast around his torso. It fit under
his shirt and was not noticeable at all. On the
first day of the term, still with the cast under his
shirt, he found himself assigned to the toughest
students in school. Walking confidently into the
rowdy classroom, he opened the window as wide
as possible and then busied himself with desk work.
When a strong breeze made his tie flap, he took
the desk stapler and stapled the tie to his chest.
He had no trouble with discipline that term.

The Lord corrects those He loves,
just as a father corrects a child in whom he delights.

PROVERBS 3:12 NLT

That energy which makes a child hard to manage is the
energy which afterward makes him a manager of life.

HENRY WARD BEECHER

Some people regard discipline as a chore.
For me, it's a kind of order that sets me free to fly.
JULIE ANDREWS

A CHILD IS...SUCH A *knot* OF
LITTLE PURPOSEFUL NATURE!

RICHARD EBERHART

If a doctor, lawyer, or dentist had forty people in his office
at one time, all of whom had different needs, and some of
whom didn't want to be there and were causing trouble,
and the doctor, lawyer, or dentist, without assistance, had
to treat them all with professional excellence for nine
months, then he might have some conception of
the classroom teacher's job.

DONALD D. QUINN

Learning is not attained by chance, it must be sought with
ardor and attended to with diligence.

ABIGAIL ADAMS

I love those who love me [wisdom];
And those who diligently seek me will find me.

PROVERBS 8:17 NASB

If you'll promise not to believe everything your child says
happens at school, I'll promise not to believe everything
he says happens at home.

A NOTE TO PARENTS

It's time to get back to some old-fashioned values,
like commitment and sacrifice and responsibility and
purity and love.... Not only will our children benefit
from our self-discipline and perseverance, but
we adults will live in a less neurotic world, too!

JAMES DOBSON

In order to manage children well, we must borrow
their eyes and their hearts, see and feel as they do,
and judge them from their own point of view.

Eugénie de Guérin

LET EVERYTHING YOU SAY
BE GOOD AND HELPFUL,
SO THAT YOUR *words*
WILL BE AN ENCOURAGEMENT
TO THOSE WHO HEAR THEM.

Ephesians 4:29 nlt

Let your words be tender and caressing...discipline that
wins the heart's assent.

Elijah Ben Solomon Zalman

When I taught in public high school for three years
I always ate lunch with a different group of students,
whether they were in my class or not, until I got to
know most of them. The teachers thought I was idiotic,
but they didn't realize that it actually made it easier
for me to teach, that before I could effectively
discipline students, I had to earn
their friendship and respect.

MARVA COLLINS

Don't demand respect.... Demand civility
and insist on honesty. Respect is something you
must earn—with kids as well as with adults.

A Passion for Knowledge

When you stood in front of our class, I could see that you not only cared about us, but you cared deeply about what you were communicating, and it was contagious.
Thank you for teaching with passion.

. . . .

Love for passing on knowledge, for the fire that
burns in the child who understands and the recognition
of a mind opened, is a priceless gift.... When I see
a young person who has a burning love for learning,
a passion for new ideas and life in general, a desire to
help others and thrive on challenges, I know I am
in the presence of a potential teacher. I would
recommend that this young person enter the
teaching profession because only in teaching
can we satisfy all of these ideals.

MARILYN JACHETTI WHIRRY

Thought flows in terms of stories—stories about events,
stories about people, and stories about intentions and
achievements. The best teachers are the best storytellers.
We learn in the form of stories.

FRANK SMITH

For everything that was written in the past
was written to teach us.

ROMANS 15:4 NIV

THE ART OF TEACHING IS THE ART OF *assisting* DISCOVERY.

MARK VAN DOREN

Among the many purposes of schooling, four stand out to
us as having special moral value: to love and care,
to serve, to empower and, of course, to learn.

ANDY HARGREAVES AND MICHAEL FULLAN

There would be no sense in asking why
if one did not believe in anything. The word itself
presupposes purpose. Purpose presupposes a powerful
intelligence. Somebody has to have been responsible.
It is because we believe in God that we
address questions to Him.

ELISABETH ELLIOT

THE LARGER THE ISLAND
OF *knowledge*, THE LONGER
THE SHORELINE OF WONDER.

RALPH W. SOCKMAN

Our progress as a nation can be no swifter than
our progress in education. The human mind is
our fundamental resource.

JOHN F. KENNEDY

Teach me knowledge and good judgment,
for I believe in Your commands.
PSALM 119:66 NIV

My greatest satisfaction as a teacher has been helping
young people learn to love history and instilling in them a
personal desire to seek knowledge. I have always seen my
role as a teacher to facilitate student learning in what will
be a life-long quest for knowledge, to help ignite in them
the spark of enlightenment, to motivate their interest,
and to cultivate their minds.

PHILIP BIGLER

I will instruct you...and guide you along the best pathway
for your life; I will advise you and watch your progress.
PSALM 32:8 TLB

The most important function of education at any level is
to develop the personality of the individual and
the significance of his life to himself and to others.

GRAYSON KIRK

A person who doesn't know but knows
that he doesn't know is a student; teach him.
A person who knows but who doesn't know
that he knows is asleep; awaken him.
But a person who knows and knows
that he knows is wise; follow him.

ASIAN PROVERB

Have a purpose in life, and having it,
throw into your work such strength of mind
and muscle as God has given you.

THOMAS CARLYLE

Learning for a Lifetime

I appreciate now how life can be a school.
Wherever I go, whatever I do, I can
learn and grow and contribute.
I learned that from you.

Through my students—over all those years—I learned
what I know about unselfish love, about laughter, about
sharing, about questioning, about honest, no-nonsense
study. I learned the joy of losing oneself in the magic of
the classroom encounter.... You will have memories that
won't stop. Your mind will have been challenged; your
values will have been forged into potent tools; you will feel
a kind of satisfaction that you did your bit for your world:
you showed up—in a most meaningful way.

BARBARA GOLEMAN

Truth, righteousness, peace, faith, and salvation
are more than words. Learn how to apply them.
You'll need them throughout your life.

EPHESIANS 6:14-15 THE MESSAGE

Anyone who stops learning is old, whether at twenty or
eighty. Anyone who keeps learning stays young.

HENRY FORD

Is life not full of opportunities for learning love?
Every man and woman every day has a thousand of them.
The world is not a playground, it is a schoolroom. Life is
not a holiday, but an education. And the one eternal
lesson for us all is how better we can love.

HENRY DRUMMOND

KNOWLEDGE IS PROUD

THAT IT KNOWS SO MUCH;
WISDOM IS *humble*

THAT IT KNOWS NO MORE.

WILLIAM COWPER

You have done many good things for me, Lord,
just as You promised.
I believe in Your commands;
now teach me good judgment and knowledge.

PSALM 119:65-66 NLT

You can teach a student a lesson for a day;
but if you can teach him to learn by creating
curiosity, he will continue the learning process
as long as he lives.

CLAY P. BEDFORD

O God, You have taught me
from my earliest childhood,
and I constantly tell others about
the wonderful things You do.

PSALM 71:17 NLT

I was still learning when I taught my last class.

CLAUDE M. FUESS